POEMS
WITH ATTITUDE+

UNCENSORED

Praise for *Poems With Attitude*

'I cannot emphasise how much every school needs this – in the library, in the classroom, for assembly, for tutorials, for PSHE, left on windowsills for the pupils to pick up – everywhere. As well as brilliant in themselves, the poems are the ideal starting point for all those awkward conversations that you know you must have, but don't know how to start – the ones on bullying, sex and drugs. In fact, I cannot emphasise how much every teenager needs this, because somewhere in this slim book is going to be the poem that they could have written.'

> – School Librarian

Praise for *Poems With Attitude: Uncensored*

'Andrew and Polly have done a remarkable job in tackling teenage preoccupations, temptations and hangups and making something aesthetically and morally strong from their hyper-honest explorations of the themes.'

> – Glasgow Herald

Other books by Andrew Fusek Peters and Polly Peters

Crash
Love, Hate and My Best Mate
Plays With Attitude: Angelcake
Plays With Attitude: Dragon Chaser

By Andrew Fusek Peters and Stephen Player

Ed and the Witchblood
Ed and the River of the Damned

POEMS

WITH ATTITUDE+

UNCENSORED

This combined edition first published in 2008
by Wayland

Poems with Attitude first published by Hodder Wayland in 2000
Poems With Attitude: Uncensored first published by Hodder Wayland
in 2002

Wayland
338 Euston Road
London NW1 3BH

Wayland Australia
Hachette Children's Books
Level 17/207 Kent Street
Sydney, NSW 2000

A CIP catalogue record for this book is available from the British
Library

ISBN 978 07502 52171

10 9 8 7 6 5 4 3 2 1

Printed in Great Britain

The paper and board used in this paperback are natural recyclable
products made from wood grown in sustainable forests. The
manufacturing processes conform to the environmental regulations of
the country of origin.

Wayland is a division of Hachette Children's Books,
an Hachette Livre UK company.

Contents

Poems With
Attitude

Andrew Fusek Peters
and
Polly Peters

WAYLAND

CONTENTS

Dedications
To Isdall School, whose year 10 booking began this collection,
and in loving memory of my brother Mark Edward Peters. A.F.P.

To John Masefield High School. P.P.

SNOGGING

snog v. & n. Brit. slang.

– v. intr. **(snogging, snogged)**. engage in kissing and caressing.

– n. a spell of snogging. [20thc: origin unkn.]

Where were the experts when it came to kissing?

Her boyfriend had broken his leg. Time to get rid of him.

She asked if *I would be the one for her.*

I lied about my age. She believed me.

I was over the moon. In fact, I was over the whole planetary solar system.

Now, I had to kiss her!

Real kissing. Not just that smack on the lips from gran stuff.

Some business to do with tongues. Oh, I knew that, tongues.

It's what we sniggered about at the bus stop . . .

Tongues touching! Revolting or what?

I couldn't remember if I'd cleaned my teeth. She was smiling,

Ready for a great big smackerooni!

I felt like James Bond with wet socks.

Can you do tongue warm ups? Lip practice?

No going back now. This was it.

I was the stone that fell off a cliff. And her lips?

Well, I know I'm being poetic really,

But they were soft like the sea and I went splash.

Wow! Mmmmm!

Now all this was wonderful, but her friends were sitting on the bed

Watching us like an experiment. Completely off-putting

There were several words I'd like to have said, but this is a
polite poem
And anyway, they were her friends.

Back to the kissing.
Technically speaking, our mouths were swapping spit,
And our tongues rolled round like wrestlers.
I found it hard to breathe.
It was great.
Five minutes went by. Then another five. Then another.
You get the picture.
Limpets were wimps compared with us.
Half an hour now.
Her eyes were closed. She seemed to be enjoying it.
I began to panic. My tongue was drowning.
What if it died?
I mean, all this kissing wasn't too bad, but I was exhausted.
Two hours later (I promise this isn't a brag, well not totally)
We finally ripped our lips apart and said goodbye.
I wandered round the town
With my tongue lolling out like a dog.
This must be love!

Unfair Fiona

On holiday in Verona,
I fancied fair Fiona,
So gorgeous now I'm blown a-
Way by thoughts of you!

But she met a boy who'd shown her
His biceps tanned with toner,
Now he's frenching my Fiona,
I'm a loner with nothing to do!

Got home and tried to phone her,
No answer for she's goin'a-
Way with that hunky moaner
On a Vespa built for two.

Farewell my false Fiona,
My heart it needs a donor,
I feel like a jilted Jonah,
Wailing and oh-so blue!

Kiss in slow motion

GLOSS APPLIER

CHAT REPLIER

FLIRT CATCHER

WINK SNATCHER

LIP CRUNCHER

POUT SCRUNCHER

MOUTH MASHER

TEETH GNASHER

TONGUE HOPPER

SALIVA SWAPPER

MOMENT'S MAN

IN THE CAN

HER ADORER

TOUCH RESTORER

STROKE SURPRISE

WIDENED EYES

HAND SNAKER

RULE BREAKER

DOWN BELOW

NO GO!

Goldilocks & the Phwoar Boys

(after: We're Going On A Bear Hunt)

We're going on a boy hunt!

We're going to catch a good one.

We're not scared!

Uh Oh! Spots!

We can't go out with them. We can't get over them.

We'll have to just cover them!

DIBBY DABBY DIBBY DABBY DIBBY DABBY SPLAT!

We're going on a boy hunt!

We're going to catch a good one.

We're not scared!

Uh Oh! Hair!

Just can't cope with it! Can't get around it!

We'll have to comb through it!

FRIZZY TANGLE FRIZZY TANGLE FRIZZY TANGLE OW!

We're going on a boy hunt!

We're going to catch a good one.

We're not scared!

Uh Oh! Breath!

Can't get over him, Can't get off with him,

Got to mouthwash!

GARGLE GURGLE GARGLE GURGLE GARGLE GURGLE BELCH!

We're going on a boy hunt!

We're going to catch a good one.

We're not scared!

Uh oh! Clothes!

Gone over everything, Can't get into it!

Have to go through them all again!

ZIP SNAP ZIP SNAP ZIP SNAP RIP!

We're going on a boy hunt!

We're going to catch a good one.

If only we dared!

Uh Oh! Make-up.

Foundation under, blusher over it,

Looking gorgeous through and through!

BRUSH BLUSH BRUSH BLUSH BRUSH BLUSH CRUSH!

We're going on a boy hunt!

We're going to catch a GREAT one.

We'll be paired!

Uh oh! Mum!

No way over this, can't get round her,

She'll see through me.

FLOUNCE SLAM FLOUNCE SLAM FLOUNCE SLAM

DAMN!

Connected

I love my dialling darling
Where roads have come to meet,
And she has got me cornered,
In the phonebox down the street.

Although it's not too roomy,
I'd recommend the view,
This palace of naughty numbers,
But the one that counts is you.

I'm afraid it's damp and drafty,
But love's a breezy catch,
I dream of our hands cupping,
The centrally heated match.

I feel like a beeping fool,
Disconnected, dumb, deranged,
Fumbling my coin of words,
Hoping for a little change.

For she has come and changed me,
It took one simple look,
And I'm desperate to receiv'er,
Don't leave me off the hook.

My eyes are frosting up now,
My heart's a broken pane,
My home the lonesome phonebox,
Under the ringing rain.

Bus Stop Date

Night makes a fog of fagsmoke
And love stains nicotine,
Each kiss dragging on our lips,
My menthol, matchless queen!

Waiting Game

Outside the swimming pool at six.

Just enough light to check my reflection, breathless, pulse
doing a four-minute mile. Lungs like bellows, fanning the fire
that blooms on my face when I see my Mum's best friend.
'Hiya Love. Waiting for a friend? Oooh, a lad is it? Nudge
Nudge!' Thank God she's gone. Look at watch. Five minutes
early. Damn. Not cool to be here first. Force hand with watch
to swim in pocket, but it's like my wrist is pushing down a
float. It just wants to pop up and keeping my arm down is like
pushing down a drowning child: Unthinkable! Whip it out and
check for signs of life. Shake. No, it hasn't stopped. But if my
watch isn't dead, then Time must be. Quick! Call an ambulance!
Time has had a heart attack. There isn't any time to lose!

Four minutes to go. Try not to look too eager. Lean against
wall and rearrange legs with all my weight on one foot. Do I
look casual enough or like a scrawny flamingo? Maybe pink
wasn't the best choice. Should I go home and change? Then I'd
be late. Though late is cool, and then he could stand and wrestle
with *his* watch. But then he might think I wasn't coming and
go home, and I'd never see him again and grow old and die

alone in a bedsit in Bangor. No, best to stay.

Three minutes. I'll saunter over and read the notices. Oh God! Didn't realise I was staring at the poster for Aqua Ante-Natal classes. Did anyone see?

Two minutes. Get back to the safety of the wall. My friend, the wall. Me and Mr Wall, tall, dark, handsome and concrete. Hanging out with a gang of bricks. Hard as houses. Yeah. Got to have something to read. Wish I'd brought a magazine. Hurray! an out of date bus timetable in the oasis of my pocket.

One minute. Check reflection. Does my hair look OK? It wasn't frizzy this morning. Zap! Pow! Biff! FRIZZ! Why can't it be curly like Katrina's? If only I had a cleavage, I'd be a knock-out! Count of ten, nine eight … Clock tower chimes the hour. Where is he then? Don't want to be seen looking out for him. Pretend there's something really interesting in my bag. He's set me up, and all the others will be laughing at me in the morning, I know it. They'll call me Kate In Wait, Sad and Snogless! It's all a big joke to him. He hates me. He hates me. He hates me. 'Oh! Hiya Matt!'

What my mother said

My mother always used to say,
When I sat sobbing at tea,
'Don't worry my girl, you're gorgeous!
And there's plenty more fish in the sea!'

'Now wave him goodbye, he's far too shallow,
Just trust, you'll have what you wish!'
'Well, thank you so much for your helpful advice,
But I couldn't get off with a fish!'

Holiday Romance

I was just twelve, and she, thirteen,
Our tongues went round like a washing machine.
Our smooching broke parental law,
A slurping kiss that left lips sore!
Romantic, adventurous holiday,
Snogging and sandcastles, if only she'd stay!
When I went home, I wrote her verse,
Her letter back was cold and terse;
Said I'd love her until the earth ends,
But she replied, 'Let's just be friends!'
And oh my heart, how it still bleeds
For Sharon Smith who lived in Leeds.

FAMILY

family n., pl. **-lies.**

1. a set of parents and children, or of relations, living together or not . . .

. . . **5.** a brotherhood of persons or nations united by political or religious features.

[ME f. L *familia* household f. *famulus* servant.]

Silence and Smiles I

I left some crumbs in the butter
A frown spread across his face.
It was teatime.
My stepdad fell utterly silent.
This was a personal insult.
The house died. No radio, no TV,
Just the song of his sighs, heaving like some ham actor.
My stomach churned.
It was almost funny.

On the fifth day,
He blessed me with his bank manager smile,
Gave me a greeting that was all sickly cream,
And I smiled back,
Desperate to please the man
Slowly curdling my mother's heart.

Smiles and Silence II

I was his little sugar and spice,
And had to call him Daddy.
He required a buttered up kiss at morning and night,
For a fifteen year old, it was creepy.

It was teatime.
I had brought home my boyfriend,
Had no desire to kiss a bogeyman.
My stepdad fell utterly silent.
This was a personal insult.
The house sighed. No radio, no TV,
Just his melodramatic breath, gasping in and out.

My boyfriend mumbled excuses and left,
Skimming off all the good feelings of the day,
Leaving me sour as old milk.

Smiles and Silence III

He had his little act off pat.
When guests turned up,
He was all voice, oily-smooth as margarine.
The door closed, he turned into a slab.
My mother moved into the spare room.

It was teatime.
The house was silent. No radio, no TV.
Every little bit of us was tidied away.
I came in, looked around,
Saw a pair of black tights sprawled across the bed
And knew, just knew he had finally strangled her.
Until I heard her car outside.

That night,
I climbed the hill above town,
A fog melting the pale yellow light,
And looked down
On the tidy houses filled with suffocating families,
And wondered if they too were practising
Smiles and silence.

The Customer

'Mind your own business!' said the wild-eyed man,
Breathing into my flabbergasted face.
'It's the holidays!' joked the wife, 'a bit of fun!
You know what kids are like, all over the place!'
She cried, carried on serving me,
Tried to hide her bruises with make up and made up lies,
As if I had not seen what I had seen:
A boy in a necklock with fear in his eyes.

I spoke up, perhaps a foolish bravery,
Me, the stupid, do-gooding customer
Then left, leaving a madman even more angry.
Later, behind blind doors, drink would father
Another punch, one son grow to know and run
Father's business, hitting his wife, beating his son.

Too Late

'Now don't come back beyond midnight.'
My only reply is to swear.
How dare she tell me what to do!
The fact is she really does care.

'And leave me the telephone number.'
I wish she'd get off my case,
But mum is concerned for her son,
Who just wants to get off his face.

When I stagger back beyond midnight,
She cries 'Can't you see that I worry?'
I try not to giggle, get out of her sight,
In the morning, perhaps I'll say sorry.

Look at my power! I've made her cry!
Now I'm a man in the making!
'I love you,' she said, but I laugh instead,
So why does my heart feel like breaking?

In the end I try to make up,
Invent some fairly white lies,
One day, I'll tell her everything,
'If only we'd talk,' she sighs.

Oh Dadless me and Sadness Mum,
Somehow we just rub along.
'We'll make the best of the worst,' she smiles
And home is where I belong.

There is no magic in him

There is no magic in him,
Only the magisterial father,
Falling like crumbled brick
To his unmuscled eyes.

There is no magic in him,
Nothing he can do right
Except to be shovelled,
Mixed up and finally tough.

At school, he stirs,
And fills the hours with 'No!'
If the system is his father,
Let it try and beat him,
Let it!

But there is no magic in the bricked up boy,
Turning away all lesson and proverb.
The Song of Solomon is sour in him,
Betrayed by fists,
He would pass on that betrayal
Before the clock struck break.

Be a fisherman,
Catch him with words, for a while.
Cast on the waters with a sweetness,
And he squirms from that uncarping touch,
Slips free the magic in him.

And the smile is a first edition,
Lips cut open in grace,
And all that is hate
Now crumbling.

But home is a phone,
Reminding him to stay in touch
With what he knows,
Where distance is a closed shop,
And the hammering of static
Beats all magic from him.

Terse Rima

(In Memory Of Frederick Maxwell Peters)

I am the thief who has taken a life!
Sang the man as he bowed most graciously,
And fell to earth, widowing his wife.

It was a case of perfect electricity,
The spark that stole you sudden as a blade,
Cutting the ties of fear and family.

My mother found you in a forest glade,
Your arms flung up as if in prayer,
Free from pain at last. But the price you paid

Was us, stolen away from cuddle and care
Sentenced to years of solitary grief,
For a husband and father no longer there.

Drink was an accomplice, the friendly thief
Who snatched my hoarded pain away.
When recovered, it was beyond belief,

A priceless hurt that came to stay.
This precious love I lack is large as life,
And every waking day is Father's day.

The Trigger (after: Blake's *The Tyger*)

STATISTIC: Ten young people of school age in the UK commit suicide each year due to being bullied

What the trigger? What the cause?
Was it words with sharpened claws?
And did the tiger smile to see
The lamb now running fearfully?

What the thought that prowled inside
The dream of doubt that never cried?
What the hammer? What the chain?
Beating out the forge of pain?

When the sick and startled stone
Made to snap the gentle bone,
What the moment? When the time,
Broke the breathing of your rhyme?

And who to shoulder your dead heart,
When you have played the final part,
Leaving those with torn out sight,
Grieving in the grove of night.

Facts and Fiction

I was told to jump by a hidden voice
Which whispered that I had no choice
To follow the footsteps of drop Dead-Dad,
Had all the requirements, stoned and sad.
I might as well give it a try,
Flap my arms, like Icarus, fly.
Dear reader, it's obvious I wasn't jolly,
But completely off my trolley.
All those years of trying to hide
Swagbags of feeling stuffed inside.
The bullies, trained in taking the peace,
Were the secret emotion police;
Arrested anyone for showing tears,
Sentenced the sensitive to years of fears.
Those voices now, I realised,
Were just the bullies, internalised.
I wrote a note that said *toodle-oo*
And shuffled up a step or two.

The fire escape led into night,

And I looked down with sudden insight.

Though my life was utterly shitty,

The mess below would not look pretty.

If this is what you contemplate,

Then take it from me, it's better to wait.

And though each day seems a pain in the arse,

Remember my friend, This Too Shall Pass.

Horse of Night

Horse of my blackest addiction,
I have felt your blood
race
the quarter mile between
my head and my heart,
and I have cheered you on,
and died at the starting gate,
and run with you,
with my heart in my mouth,
my whole body
miles down the road,

and I have collapsed,
spent
at the broken gate
you crossed
to gain your freedom,
and you dragged me on,
on a race no one could win,
racing for racing's sake,
racing until your hard, proud,
black veins pumped dry,

and the sun
and moon
bowed to your hard body,
and today is tomorrow
and I am racing still.

By Mark Peters (1961–1993)

For Mark

For when my brother dies,
I shall cry tears of stone,
Never will I have felt so alone
And my heart will try to be hard.

For when my brother dies,
No more late-night Monopoly and after
Bacon and eggs with a cup of laughter,
The yolk of dawn just breaking.

For when my brother dies,
I shall cry a city of tears
Then put on a smile, hide all my fears,
If only I could, if only.

For when my brother dies,
No more hate and family spite,
Now I'm fine, everything's all right
But I will miss the making up.

For when my brother dies,
I shall cry blades of grass,
People will be polite, dare not ask
Why my garden overgrows.

For when my brother dies,
I shall have no brother,
No other to hug and to hold
And I the younger
am the one who will grow old.

High up in the Hills

High up in the hills
The wind is blowing my brother away.
He is going away now
As if he was just popping out to the shops
As if he just put the phone down
As if he went for a walk and just carried on.

I remember the tale of the Alcoholic who told his wife
He was just slipping out for a packet of cigarettes
And wasn't seen for five years.

My brother is not migrating like a bird
Nor is he folding over the world like the moon,
To grow thin, disappear and come back new again.
He is no fairy tale
For in the story, they live happily ever after.

He doesn't have a writer's block.
There is nothing more to write
And all there is between us are the memories we made.
So shall the days go.

He is dying of Aids.

But who is there to aid him in this death?

A midwife for life . . .

Who shall bring him out? Who shall give death to him?

Ease him in his labours, his dying pains?

Who shall husband him, mother to him, hold him?

And shall he cry out like a newborn babe?

Cry out against the shortness of his years,

The tight span he squeezed to the last breath

That ended by squeezing him?

No answers,

For answers only come at the end.

And no one is going the whole way with him.

It is his death. He must own it.

He must die it.

And if there is light,

Why is it so full of darkness?

And if there is faith,

Why can I only question?

And if there is peace,

Give him some,

That he may sleep.

FRIENDS

friend n. **1.** a person known well to another and regarded with liking, affection, and loyalty; an intimate. **2.** an acquaintance or asssociate. **3.** an ally in a fight or cause, supporter. **4.** a fellow member of a party, society, etc. **5.** a patron or supporter: a friend of the opera **6. be friends (with).** to be friendly (with). **7. make friends (with).** to become friendly (with). ~vb. **8.** (tr). an archaic word for **befriend**.

[Old English *freond;* related to Old Saxon *friund,* Old Norse *frandi,* Gothic *frijonds,* Old High German *friunt*]

Sometimes it's all so amazing

Sometimes, it's all so amazing,
I could fall at the feet of every singing pigeon.
Shopkeepers' conversations seem positively Shakespearean
And the sweet wrappers that flower down the street
Are perfectly arranged.

Sometimes, it's all so amazing,
I could watch a tree like a TV,
Every leaf an amazing documentary,
Each shadow riveting as a World Cup final.

Sometimes, it's all so amazing,
I'd say kind things to people I can't even stand,
Look for the good in their face, heart and hand,
And find it.

Sometimes, it's all so amazing,
Every day becomes a holy day,
I could even pray to bacon and eggs!
And a cup of tea is a spiritual experience.

Sometimes, it's all so amazing,
I could say hello to a complete stranger,
Let go my forever fear of danger,
And just for a second he would become my deepest friend.

The Horror, the Horror!

Out to my mate's for a night in, that's terminally groovy,
Got loads of crisps and coke in for the x-cert horror movie.
Give us a gory giggle (Yeah!), and snorts of sudden surprise,
For the close up, slowed down scene, where they gouge out
each of his eyes!
We never turn away (No Way!), nor hold our popcorn breath,
As we love spurting blood (Hooray!) and dollops of dastardly death!
Cycling home at the end's alright, except for the dark bike shed,
Where a psycho waits just out of sight, to slowly remove my head!

He and she

We were best friends, a fit like kettle to cup,
And the boiling need to brag and boast was poured away.
We talked as fast as a racing horse, every word a winner.
I dug into my pocketed fears,
A kid showing his precious marbles,
But the only thing she laughed at was my doubt.
She praised my sky-scraping dreams,
High rise hopes in a young head.

One night, we wandered backstreets,
Infatuated with neon, addicted to architecture.
Tipsy with talking, we swayed through busy avenues,
'Til we came to a churchyard crushed in a corner.
All was sweet and silent,
Save for the murmur of a million shifting feet.
An old street lamp splashed yellow into shadow.
A fat oak tree squatted like a leafy Buddha,

And gravestones kept themselves to themselves,
Their stone epitaphs seeping into green.
We sat on the wall, between present and past,
Best friends for now and for now and forever now,
Where the cobbles were pearls beneath our feet.

Perfect Blend

She's a:

Sadness safe-cracker,

A down-in-the-dumps hijacker.

A deepest secret keeper,

A talk-for-hours non-sleeper.

An automatic advice dispenser,

A future candidate for Mensa.

An Olympic-qualifying talker,

A hold-head-high-whatever walker.

A listener to all my woes,

A fear-of-God to all my foes.

A promise fulfiller, gossip killer,

Dance-all-nighter, tiredness fighter,

Solid shoulder for things I've told her.

She's my:

Round the bend, got to spend

Quick to lend, own trend

Perfect blend

Best friend!

(what would I do without her?)

1 Slugs & Snails & Puppy Dogs' Tails

Lads like football, lads like cars,

Lads like hanging round in bars.

Lads fart to start up conversations

And hang in gangs at railway stations.

Lads show off by acting tough,

And don't know when they've drunk enough.

Lads love lager with designer labels,

But end up legless under tables.

Lads like playing contact sport,

And wear the socks their mothers bought.

Lads play rugby, lads play pool,

But often don't do well at school.

Lads wear T-shirts when it's chilly

With no idea that they look silly.

Lads can't cook and Lads can't sew,

They'd rather sit and watch grass grow.

Lads, you know, are king-sized rats

However I can tell you that's

A load of crap from where I'm sitting,

'Cos I'm a lad who's into knitting!

2 Sugar & Spice & all things nice

Girls are sugary, girls are spicy,

Girls like trainers that are pricy.

Girls like pink and fluffy stuff,

Girls are sweet and don't act tough.

Girls wear high-rise, platform heels,

Girls theorise on how love feels.

Girls like boys, and girls like dates,

Girls like shopping with their mates.

Girls keep secrets from their mums,

And like to eye up cute boys' bums.

Girls like talk that lays souls bare,

Girls like to style each other's hair.

Girls are friends 'til death do part,

But steal their bloke and you're a tart!

Girls like gossip, girls like bitching,

Snipping friendship's careful stitching.

Girls compare who they have kissed,

Girls can wound without their fist.

Girls read books about romance,

And step round handbags when they dance.

But this girl thinks this list is barmy,

'Cos she's just off to join the army!

Bullying

bully ~n., pl. **-lies. 1.** a person who hurts, persecutes, or intimidates weaker people. **2.** *Archaic.* a hired ruffian. **3.** *Obsolete.* a procurer; pimp. **4.** *Obsolete.* a fine fellow or friend. **5.** *Obsolete.* a sweetheart; darling. ~vb. **-lies, -lying,-lied. 6.** (when tr., often foll. by *into*) to hurt, intimidate, or persecute (a weaker or smaller person), esp. to make him do something. ~adj. **7.** dashing; jolly: *my bully boy.* **8.** *Informal.* very good; fine. ~interj **9.** Also: **bully for you, him,** etc. *Informal.* well done! bravo!

[C16 (in the sense: sweetheart, hence fine fellow, hence swaggering coward): probably from Middle Dutch *boele* lover, from Middle High German *buole,* perhaps childish variant of *buroder* BROTHER)

Remembrance Day

When we have left our school in peace,
Does bullying's shellshock ever cease?
Here's a rollcall, the sensitive few,
Names called out in the blameless crew:
Mandy the fat one, without any hope,
At last succeeded with a length of rope;
Yaseen, shamed for her boot-black skin,
A gallon of bleach did her in;
James, too posh for the common attack,
Went over the top with a hit of smack;
Martin Martini, skinny git,
Gave up eating for the hell of it.
Thanks to the bullies, bayonet in hand,
Leaving us in No-Man's Land,
Privates fighting private thought,
Trying to ignore what we've been taught.
And me? Retreated in the warmth of dope,
Got too blown away to cope,
Wondering what the hell it's for,
Limping, survived the mindless war.

Now, I am a veteran, visiting schools,
Who doesn't take kindly to thuggish fools.
They think it's a gas, don't see that their fun
Is the equivalent of a loaded gun.
I'm so sick of sickos taking the piss,
Deserting their conscience in cowardice,
Leaving the lost ones with lonely fears,
Trudging the trenches of tear-sodden years.

Ray

Summer thinks he's a lad,
Though it's all a flowery farce
In fact when he drinks, he's a total rain
And the sun shines out of his grass.

Unevensong (sung by the stupid)

To the tune of: What shall we do with the drunken sailor?

What shall we do with Duncan Taylor?
What shall we do with Duncan Taylor?
What shall we do with Duncan Taylor
Early in the morning?

Hoo-ray and up he rises!
Life is full of cruel surprises!
And we're several sizes
Bigger than him this morning!

Lock him up in the classroom cupboard!
Lock him up in the classroom cupboard!
Lock him up in the classroom cupboard!
To serve him as a warning!

What shall we do with Duncan Taylor
Now he's become a stinking wailer?
This is the life of a teenage jailer,
Early in the morning!

Laugh at him when he starts to weep,
Got what he asked for, little creep,
Can't say that I'll lose any sleep,
When I rise in the morning!

What shall we do now he's sunken paler,
Call him a sissy girly failure,
Works too hard, it's time to nail 'her',
Serves him right for fawning!

Laugh until our guts are aching,
Stupid prat what a racket he's making,
By God it's fun to be taking
The rise in the early morning!

Hoo-ray and up he rises
Life is full of cruel surprises
And we're several sizes
Bigger than him this morning.

Bruises Heal

Names, cold shoulders,
Silence in the canteen;
Her words are scalpels,
Cutting self esteem.

"Stuck up little cow!
Thinks she's really it!'
Laughter slices, she prescribes
A sharp, unfunny wit.

Ridiculed for standing out,
My marks are much too high
And so she drip-feeds saline hate,
Injecting with a lie.

She's bright, she'll find
The weakest spot to pierce and prod and poke.
She uses stealth, and poisoned words
And wears them like a cloak.

It seems I am her favourite game
And I'm the one who loses,
If she'd done this with her fists,
At least there would be bruises.

Camp Concentration

At school, if your hair was too long,
Or if you weren't particularly strong,
If you were sensitive to names,
Or quiet, or not into games,
They called you *bent, poof, queer*
And gave you the gift of a life of fear.
Once their limited vocabulary was spent,
Not fitting in, you were branded different.
These childish rules equally applied
If you were fat, or thin, or easily cried,
Or white, black, brown, not part of the race.
Losers, wore glasses on their face.

The Nazis came from that same school,
For them it was a gas to apply the rule,
Narrow-minded, upright, straight,
Twilight thugs, handing out hate.
My mum, when twelve, in Prague one night,
Had the SS search her room by torchlight,
Boots so high they reached above the bed,
'Looking for resisters,' they said,
As they took her school friend far away,
On a camping trip that none would choose.
I have friends who are gay,
My mum had friends who were Jews.

'Waiter there's a thug in my salad!'

I'm an apple,

Used to hang round with a bunch of grapes.

The Hard Bunch, but they all ended up as winos.

Now I'm in the apple gang.

Wanna be in my gang?

For a start, we don't like oranges.

Any orange that gets in our way,

We squash! You should see them run!

Lemons? Yellow through and through,

Not as tough as me or you.

Lychees? Oh please!

They're a funny colour, and they're foreign.

Go back to Lychee Land.

Bananas? You must be bananas!

Fruit cakes all of them! Bender Boys.

Don't wanna get mixed up with that bunch.

Pineapple? What can you say?

I mean, zits or what!?

You could almost peel her skin.

She needs help badly!

Onion? What are you doing here?

Don't you know you don't belong?

Send for the doctors!

He's a total vegetable case!

Who does that leave?

Melony Melonbrain,

She's a pain, she's too fat,

Too soppy, too sweet

And she's soft in the head.

I think you're better off dead, my dear.

Pears? My older brother's a pear!

So pears are alright! Alright?

In fact, he's so hard,

He'd have YOU for breakfast any day!

'Cos I'm a happy apple with all my apple friends.

If you wanna belong,

Don't be a lemon, or a stupid melon!

Just put on an apple skin and sing my apple song!

Apple! Apple! Apple! Oi! Oi! Oi!

Apple! Oi! Apple! Oi!

Apple! Apple! Apple!

Oi! Oi! Oi!

Building Blocks

I have been built out of bullies,
With insults they moulded me.
For a while I walled up my fears,
And hid myself in poetry.

The house of books where I wandered,
In rooms of brain-bright thought,
Sheltered me brick by tender brick,
And the hateful words they taught

I caught and made my own
confident concrete tower,
To look down on the bullies,
For the pen is a mighty power.

They laughed at the sensitive boy.
And his guttering, spluttering tears,
But bottled up bullies get old and cold,
As they blunder the lonely years.

Oh bully boys that built me,
Don't you know that girls find appealing
Not louts who love to get plastered,
But boys filled up with feeling?

Yes, I was the prat that was good for a laugh,
The skinny old git, the swot.
Now I'm living my life with a beautiful wife,
Free from the bully dry rot.

So thank you, bullies that built me,
With all your crumbling hate,
Out of this mess, came a success,
And a man who has mastered his fate.

Sexuality

SEXUAL adj. 1. of or relating to sex, or to the sexes
or the relations between them.

2. *Bot.* (of classification) based on the distinction of sexes
in plants.

3. *Biol.* having a sex.

sexuality n. **sexually** adv.

[LL *sexualis* (as sex)]

Girl Talk

Now most people think that a poem might deal
With the shimmering swaying of trees,
So a subject you may not expect in a verse
Is sexually transmitted disease.

Discomfort! Shock horror! You can't discuss that!
We want love poems, something romantic!
But horror and shock are inadequate words
If it's you who are suddenly frantic.

Diseases with names I can't even spell
Are more common than most people know.
And a sudden encounter, an intimate match,
Is all that they need to grow.

In the heat of the moment, when starting to feel
Swayed by his shimmering eyes,
Remember that trees are never immune
From being cut down to size.

Remember the brother who couldn't be bothered
With barriers or thoughts of protection.
He just wanted some fun at the party, and thus
Gave that virus a welcome reception.

A dearly loved son, a brother, a boyfriend,
A lad who adored pretty maids.
'Cut down in his prime,' wept his friends, when they heard
Of the loss in his fight against Aids.

Now trees have hundreds and thousands of seeds
And a mission to multiply,
'But I'm not a tree! It won't happen to me!'
Is the stupidest kind of lie.

So if it's your choice and you've made up your mind.
Don't leave this decision to luck,
If he won't use a condom, ignore all his charms and
Forget it, he ain't worth a . . .

Diagrammatic

My mum gets dead embarrassed
By my questions, which have her floored.
She told me that a diaphragm was:
'What the teacher draws on the board!'

I shouldn't have asked my dad,
With his terrible sense of timing,
But at dinner he tried to explain
That tampons were 'essential for climbing.'

I asked my mum about the pill,
And was it dangerous to take?
She shook her head, then smiled and said:
'It's great for a bad headache!'

Oh meet my ignorant family,
Repressive, evasive and quiet,
For this girl, it's about bloody time
To start an Awareness Riot!

Nothing to prove

It was a case of tender lust, when talk turned to touch,
Her detecting fingers gently fussed,
Forgave my frantic fumbling clutch
In case of tender lust.

My mum was out, her bed became a must,
Our sighs were sirens, nothing was too much,
Until the springs surrendered,
The bed was bust!

Her words dissolved my impotent fears. Such
Love now sentenced me to trust,
Jailing doubt as out of touch
To close the case of tender lust.

PS: My mum is still annoyed about the bed!!!

Gas Mark 16

I'm really tired of being told about sex
By ancient, mouldy, pain in the necks.
If it's so bad, how come I find,
That certain thoughts keep crossing my mind?
And adults do it, but never say,
Else how did I get here anyway, eh?
But boys are bad, with their wicked wiles,
Their lying hands and deceiving smiles.
I won't be served with this stereotype,
Send it away with its overdone hype!
For love is a recipe, followed with care,
Seasoned with feeling and flamed until rare,
And whether they're fast-food fish and chips,
Or a slow-cooked tender steak, relationships
Don't have to be a drunken alley slam,
Or a five-minute fumbling Wham Bam.
And don't worry, we're not all dumb,
I've taken advice as a rule of thumb,
Protection's a starter that saddles this horse,
Before we ride out to the main course.
Then there's time to enjoy and explore –
The secret of the adults' swinging door
That they want to keep slammed shut.

But I am not some adolescent smut –
Obsessed lad (though, maybe that's a lie!),
Corrupting girls with a wink and a sigh,
Nor am I some deadly depraved beast,
But merely a beginner at life's fruitful feast
So come on, give us a break, don't quibble,
Just because I crave a natural nibble!

What goes on in boys' heads

Oh Tanya, my darling tomato-haired totty
I tried to Ketchup, but you gave me the slip.
In my dreams you are saucy and ripe for some hotty,
But then you turned round and gave me the pip.

Pressure

Have you? Haven't you?

Do you? Don't you?

Will you? Won't you?

Who is going to?

Peer Pressure, Peer Pressure

It could be fags, it could be fashion,

Could be drugs, it could be passion.

Peer Pressure, Peer Pressure

Love it, loathe it, like it, hate it,

No escape, must just await it.

Peer Pressure, Peer Pressure

Boys, they have to brag they've scored,

Build the lie 'til mates applaud.

Fears Pressing, Fears pressing

Girls get stuck in two way traps

In murky mazes without maps.

Jeers Press Her, Jeers Press Her

If she does, she's called a slag,

And rumours build with tongues that wag.

Peer Precipice, Peer Precipice

But if she doesn't, which is worse?

'Tight Bitch!' is the poisoned curse.

Sheer Pressure, Sheer Pressure

But, we're given brains to reason things,
Don't have to wait for what fate brings.
Clearly Precious, Clearly Precious
We have a mind, we have a choice,
We have an individual voice,
No need to put your life on loan,
It's no one's choice except your own.
Peer Pressure, Peer Pressure
Peer Pressure EXPLODES!

Mind Pollution

Though the hairstyle resembled an oil spill,
His chatup, well slick was the word.
But his bragging was crude as he went for the kill
And fouled this particular bird.

If only he'd talk to her once in a while,
Instead of just dropping his anchor,
A lumbering vessel without any style,
Now he's known as an absolute tanker.

Statistic: '70% of young women regret their first sexual experience'

It was way back in the sixties:
A right was battled and won,
By women who fought for freedom of choice
Beyond that of mother or nun.

Now we're forty years further,
But more trapped than ever, it seems
For belief in choice has broken
Like the mirror of childhood dreams.

For the right to say 'Yes' got hijacked,
Somewhere along the way,
To become just a foregone conclusion
No discussion, no choices, no say.

And it's 'Loaded minx, She's desperate for sex!
Read all about it inside!'
And, 'Be one of us!' the insidious chant,
'Don't end up on the opposite side.'

Perhaps it's time for a different cause,
A fight for the right to say 'No.'
And to be well informed, learn more about choice,
And to know that it's fine to go slow.

It's active choice that should be the crusade,
Responsible, reasoned and yours,
Not passive, or pressured, assumed or presumed,
For you hold the key to those doors.

Information is power, it means you can choose
The right person, right time and right place.
Then there are no regrets for you've opted to take
The slow journey, and not the fast race.

Easy

He swaggers downstairs and stops
To see who might be looking, hesitates
And joins a group who loll against the wall;
Drags attention from a fag burn in the carpet
By dramatic adjusting of his shirt,
Then squats. 'Got a fag?' he asks,
Grinning deliberately, willing them
One of them, to ask: 'Where is she then?'
Only a slight exhalation indicates relief at being asked.
Slowly, he draws a breath,
Like the drumroll preceding the high wire act
And rolls his eyes.
'Upstairs y'know. Sortin' herself out.'
And he smiles a lazy smile
And hooks his thumbs in belt loops,
Stage whispers, 'First time y'know: hers, not mine of course.'
And his audience lean back appreciatively.
'Where's that fag then? Gotta light?' Deep drag now.
'Well, yeah, bit of a slag, but a goer. Oh yeah! A real goer.'
They are reeled in, staring and envious.
'Did you really?'
'Oh yeah, too right!' . . .

While upstairs,
Mascara tears
Rain black
Into the basin.

Booze & Drugs

booze *n. & v. colloq.*

-*n.* **1.** alcoholic drink. **2.** the drinking of this (on the booze).

-*v. intr.* drink alcoholic, liquor, esp. excessively or habitually.

[earlier *bouse, bowse,* f. MDu. *busen* drink to excess]

drug -*n.* **1.** any synthetic or natural chemical substance used in the treatment, prevention, or diagnosis of disease. Related adj.: **pharmaceutical. 2.** a chemical substance, esp. a narcotic, taken for the pleasant effects it produces.

[C14: from Old French *drogue,* probably of Germanic origin]

The Pearls of Primrose Hill

That night, her son got drunk,
Stole a bike and wove his way
In giggling stitches through the fraying streets.
The leather-black air was sharp,
And his breath, a swaying incense
As he prayed to the god of speed.

He hit the hill at sixty,
And took to the trees in a slalom,
Wild boy-rider, tilting at windmills,
Mistook a bin for his enemy and charged.
Took flight,
True as the compass needle,
Dead-head butted the unforgiving litter.
His front teeth burst like buttons,
Limp as cloth, he fell to the ground.
Thank god for Anaesthetic Alcohol,
His mouth a rose now blooming with blood,
The ragdoll son crawled home.

His mother was waiting, waiting
Waiting all the long and solemn night.
When she saw him,
It punctured her pincushion heart.
She sped him in a hurry to the hospital,
Where experts informed her that teeth could be saved.

At the comedown of dawn,
The sudden grey woman
Crawled through dogshit grass,
Carrying such unbelievable grief
As she searched the hill for needles in the haystack,
The precious pearls of her son's smashed teeth.

On Hampstead Heath

The moon is round as our wide eyes.
We lounge in the living room of grass,
With friends as soft, breathing pillows,
And flickering lights of the city below
The image we are glued to.
Fresh picked mushrooms mash in our mouths,
Mixing with jokes and salty whispers.
Joints passed like salt and pepper,
Condiments for conversation.
We breathe in honeysuckle, roses, stocks;
Hold the high until our lungs almost burst with the
Scent of summer.

Night grows deep as thought,
We are dozy starlings, anxious for the nest.
We slip into the tarmac river with our skateboards,
Swoop and slalom down hills with a hiss,
Past dumb cars, shut-eyed windows and
Lamps drowsily nodding their heads.
We lean into corners and turn, the wheeling flock
Moving like mercury
As we tumble into the valleys
Of fumbling locks and stumbling stairs
And the easy contentment of sleep.

War Story

Couldn't find a vein, what the heck,
Stuck the needle in my neck.
Felt the beaming sun fantastic,
Heart slowed down, eyes elastic.
Hours of nodding, gouging out,
One of the gang raised up a shout:
'Oh dear, O'Malley's OD'd!' she said.
He wasn't just pale, but rather dead.
'What shall we do with him now?' she cried.
With totally smacked out brains we tried
To think of a plan that was truly cunning,
Though all we felt like doing was running.
We said a little junkie prayer,
Then rolled him up in a rug threadbare.
The house was a wreck, the builders' chute
Provided an excellent exit route.
I'm afraid that while we giggled away,
O'Malley slipped down like a fast bob-sleigh,
And landed, crashed out in a council skip.
It was that kind of relationship.

I'm ashamed to admit that we found it a scream,
And O'Malley? Gone like a darkening dream.

Black

It was night. We were stoned with lagered-up skinheads
On the roof of the shell of a squat
In the warm summer city.
Our laughter rippled,
Though the friends-of-a-friend thugs in boots and braces
Seemed too quiet.
The youngest started it, demanding our dope.
Not more than thirteen,
Face smooth as a chilling cherub
He swung his pendulum fist.
My brother's white shirt turned red,
A magic trick gone wrong,
His head dealt blow after blow from the pack.
I curled into the corner, a fragile new moon,
And the pounding made me see stars;
Their grunts and our groans, sounded almost pornographic,
But my only desire was to fly.
Adrenaline grew me wings,
I soared from the screaming roof.
Neighbours stayed quiet behind a flock of locks -
As I landed, ran through the light-shy lanes
Desperate for mum.

For years after,

I escaped into Kung-Fu movies,

Imagined I'd been training since I was six,

Relished encounters where gangs were wiped out

With a flick of a finger

And an enigmatic smile on my boyish face.

Fag Off

When at school,

Fags were cool.

Not so young,

Removed right lung.

Hacking got to me,

Tracheotomy.

Ignore that boffin!

Carry on coffin'.

Finally led

To a boxed in bed,

Nobody's fool,

I'm now *dead* cool.

The Night Kitchen

The Mohican has lost his America.
His hair cuts the air like a scythe.
Tonight is his night.
He stoops in the subway and finds ten pounds,
Hey! Food and fags and glue,
To stick together what has fallen apart inside.

He squats in Islington,
Burning furniture for fuel,
Squeezes his glue into a plastic bag,
Then like the horse this Indian never rides,
He puts his face to the trough
And snorts the heady fumes.
His mane quivers, eyes roll,
Radios blare in Pentecostal tongue
And the fire is in his head.

Mohican canters into the streets,
Searches out oases dead by day
And breathes in the midnight hour.
Offices have closed their mouths,
Are dumb to the shifters and shufflers,

And Mohican, eyes spinning like plates,
Juggles legs and arms in the effort to remain upright.

Night is swift as lark,
And sharp shop windows filled with women bring no comfort.
There is nothing to be had,
But the comedown of the moon,
Sagging like an old breast,
And the mole stars fading in the twilight.

Cleaners come in trucks, on foot
To fill the silent city with broom and bustle.
Curtains itch. Alarms declare bad jokes.
And the coffee shops reveal a drinking hole.
Mohican slows his trot to a walk and seats himself in the saddle
of caffeine.
The rising of the sugar salmon
He slips out,
Lost in the singing crowd,
Moving against that rush hour ride,
Searching for the source in what dark spring.

Pub-erty

It wasn't all fights and vomit and death.
To be tall was a blessing. Take a deep breath,
Walk up to the bar, and ask for a drink,
Landlord sees boy with bottle, doesn't blink,
But pulls the pint, and I set up, set sail
Fifteen, skinny as a yard of ale.
Sudden found friends, and spilling ease,
I was part of the gang on the high seas
Of lager, laughter, perched on my girl's knee,
In the harbour, safe from her storming family.
The evil that got her dad was not *this* drink
That he hid in bottles under the sink.
This couldn't be the stuff we swore we would not touch,
But glue that bound us, careless crutch
Of liquid warmth on winter nights,
Gambling the fruits and flashing lights,
Far, far away from drowning school,
As we dived on cue into games of pool.

When the bell rang, like froth we poured
Into the streets, suddenly cold and bored,
Tipsy weavers, threading the gloom,
Headed with take-outs for somebody's room,
And dancing, kissing, gulping down fun.
The black and tan night only just begun.

Bored

When I was a teenage thug,
Before I discovered the arts,
We'd hang around the bikesheds,
Smoke fags, and light our farts.

Blow-Back

Grass, Blow, Dope and Spliff,
Red Leb and oily Black,
These are the words that turn you on,
To a night out on the crack.

Bong, chillum, paraphernalia,
Pipes and skins galore,
Laugh, giggle, got the munchies,
Rolling round the floor.

Boy with hash has instant mates,
Whose smiles are filled with lies,
Shallow hero of the night,
With double-glazing eyes.

Strangers, nonsense, garbled words,
Head bent over the loo,
Rush slowed down to a sickly trickle,
Spaced out, splash and spew.

Got so high, went into orbit,
Planets of pills to pep me,
Hot sweats, visions, paranoia,
Police are out to get me.

All this fun for the price of a toke,
That made me a real hard lad,
But in the end I lost the joke
And went completely mad.

Oh people who take drugs are cool,
In school, they've got street cred,
But personally, there's more to life,
Than ending up dull or dead.

Icarus Sickarus

I was nervous,
They suggested a drink
Gave in, said yes, didn't think.

I felt less shy,
They said you could try
One puff of this, and boy you'll fly!

I was gliding,
Didn't take heed,
When they said Sniff this! you'll be up to speed.

I took off
Towards the sun,
Burn this! they hissed, It's a ball of fun!

I took it,
Until I could take no more,
Suddenly began to soar,

The sky was melting
I jumbled my words,
That fell like tumbling come-down birds.

I crashed,

And suddenly woke to find,

I had mashed the wings of my mind.

Sniffing for glues

Give a squeeze

Liquid frees

In the bag

Make me gag

Such perfume

Head goes ZOOM

Sticky nose

Vision grows

Sky rise hum

Down I come

Thirteen floors

Thunder roars

End of story

Rather gory

Mad for it

I could not get used to the habit,
My mind worn away with using,
Lost in the waves and foaming mad,
Too far from Normality Shore,
Stuck in Sargassos of saddening weed,
As the tide shut me off like a door.

I was too shy to walk through the door,
As a youth, had developed a nervous habit,
Until I was offered a toke of weed,
Could not be seen to be refusing,
One puff, and Wow, I felt so sure,
Confidence soared, I talked like mad.

Bullies are puffed up and mad
On fear, So I hid as a kid behind the door,
Hoping for a teacher to reassure
Me. They didn't. I was left to inhabit
A school where hate was a musing
Scythe to cut this pathetic weed.

So I became best mates with weed,
It grew in me and I grew madder,

Blossomed into dark abusing.
The Lord of Hash was the one to adore,
I prayed at the shrine in my punk-rocker habit,
Visioning monk of the cocksure.

On one last trip I left that shore,
So stoned, I lost control, weed
Myself, shat the floor, was led to the habit
Of hospitals, and wards of the wingless mad,
Lived in fear of the locking door
Could only mutter, 'It's so confusing,'

Over and over, all thoughts fusing
Into a lump of black. I tried to shore
Up my sanity, but the greedy Jackdaw
Had stolen sense to feather his widow-weed
Nest. Me the March hare, dancing mad,
Broken down, shuffling out of habit.

This was the joy of using weed,
A boy marooned on the maddening shore,
At last his habit of dope unhinged him,
slamming shut the hopeful door.

Is there life after drugs?

Without the drugs I felt naked and raw,
Unsure of winning this personal war.
I wouldn't go back, but couldn't see,
That getting clean was victory.
I remember once, stoned on a train,
Overheard this couple, with half a brain,
Talking about how drugs were boring,
As they stared into each other's adoring
Eyes. It made me want to puke, and how
I laughed at those poor saddos. Now
I fit this anorak myself,
Have left the pills on memory's shelf.
The first time I made love, in fear
And lack of faith, I tanked myself on beer
And rolled a spliff with shaking fingers.
This is the image that lingers;
No girl had seen me naked before,
Would she laugh at what she saw?
Thank God that fear was left unfounded,
Only my out-of-it brain was confounded.
Life today without the boozy bandage
Is much more fun. Perhaps it's age,
But somehow pissed-up Friday nights,

The blur of clubs and lure of neon lights,

The chat ups, the endless mindless mumbling,

The stagger, the sway, the feel up fumbling

Is over, done. When I was barking, out of my tree

Friends and future were a fantasy.

Easier to fly on feather white coke,

And laugh at life's great big bloody joke.

So off my head, I nearly lost the thread.

Friends of mine succeeded, wound up dead

Cool? No, truly cool is taking a toke of life, a puff

Of late night love is more than enough.

Sometimes I laugh so much, I'm totally gone,

And strangers ask what is he on?

Nothing mate. The world is my upper,

I'll do without that liquid supper.

Jacked up with hope for the days ahead

I chase the dragon of my dreams, instead.

To Eileen Armstrong and the pupils at Cramlington High
School. Thanks for fantastic feedback!

POEMS With ATTITUDE
UNCENSORED

Andew Fusek Peters
and
Polly Peters

WAYLAND

Contents

LOVE

WITHIN SPITTING DISTANCE

Pucker those lips,
prepare to dive,
Brush those teeth 'til they feel alive,
Take a breath, fill up your lungs,
Ready for the race of teenage tongues.
Round and round like a washing machine,
Until you encounter Nick O'Teen.
By gum, it's time to stop and think
And ban his brain-dead, bad-breath stink.
Admit it girl, it wouldn't go far,
Chuck him out and say tar-tar!
The race is lost, this boy's a mutt,
Who wants to snog a cigarette butt?

TRENCH TACTICS

IN THE NO-MAN'S LAND outside the loos,
Opposing camps are drawn up
Rude rumours have flown.
Boy then girl pushed forward.
First shots are fired.
'Fancy a movie?'
'Suppose.'
They retreat to their ranks to interrogate
The code of flashing eyes and mumbled
  response.
Later that night:
The sentry guides them with torchlight
To velvet trenches.
The film begins with a barrage of sound
  and light
And the boy's arm lumbers like a tank over
  the back of the chair
To land on the enemy's shoulder.
Yes! Yes! Yes!
He has entered the bottle zone.

Her head swivels. He moistens his tongue.
  She swallows spit.
They engage. ATTACK! ATTACK!
  IT'S A HEART ATTACK!
Teeth clash like armour plating.
Spit bombs fly between mouths.
Necks are targeted with biting precision.
His wounded tongue (he bit it earlier through
  nerves)
Responds to resuscitation.
Mates whoop while punters
Tut-tut like machine-gun fire.

What was the movie about? Who cares?
They troop out into the night.
Neck wounds dressed with scarves
To foil spying parents.
This was SNOGGING FOR VICTORY!

TURN-TABLE

'You must be tired, love!'
'Why?' I say,
''Cos you've bin runnin' thru' me mind all day!
And your dad's a burglar, stealing stars!
He must 'ave bin all the way to Mars!'
'Why's that?' I ask in mock surprise.
'To stick 'em in your sparklin' eyes!'
He leers, and leans against the doors
I raise my eyes in silence, pause.
'Get your coat, you've pulled!' I smile,
Now watch him run a minute mile!

THE PERFECT LAD

The lad for me has teeth so white,
It's obvious he's Mr Right;
He'll know that I have got a brain,
'Let's talk!' will be his main refrain,
And not about the sporting score,
But **feelings, poetry,** and more.
His hands won't head towards my skirt,
He'll even cry when he is hurt.
He'll change his boxers every day,
His biceps! Oh, they'll make me sway!
He'll have such perfect, spotless skin,
His clothes will not be out, but in.
But such a lad is just a rumour,
I'll make do with a sense of humour.

SKATE DATE

This the day that anything can happen.
I have embarked on my skateboard
And am soaring over this blue summer
At a cruising altitude of ten centimetres.
My heart is in take-off.
Got a number in my pocket.
A phone in my bag and a date in my turbulent head.
This is the day that anything can happen.
All in a moment.
In the school corridor, with a blush
That bloomed on my face like an unsure flower,
My mates egging me on,
And me scrambled up with fear,
I stuttered one simple question
While praying for the answer.
And for once, on the day that anything could happen,
It did.

No Sod-Off-Saddo snigger,
No Got-To-Be-Kidding-Oh-Well-Life's-A-Pile-Of-
  Crap-Anyway,
No-Heads-Together-and-Giggle-When-They-See-Me
But the sweetest 'Sure!' I ever heard and a flash
  of eyes
And now I am sky high,
Cruising this blue summer of day,
Negotiating pavements perfectly,
The road running like a dark river,
Carrying me, with a number in my pocket,
A phone in my bag
And my heart beating like a ring tone
On the day that anything can happen.

LOVE TRIANGLE

He says it's 'cos I feel rejected!
Pray his privates be bisected! May his spots
  be multiplied
And his swagger sub-divide.
It isn't hard to calcluate
The adding up of all my hate:
Subtract regret and add derision
Forever between us, Long Division.
Who cares what planet he was on?
As for me? Well, Polygon.

BRACE YOURSELF

Now call us a pair of anoraks
Sporting identical train tracks
When we smooch, our steel-capped faces
Make sparks fly thanks to our braces
But now I'm going really mental
'Cos my boyfriend's orthodental.
As we furnurkled, just my luck,
That this snogging got us stuck!
An hour's canoodling I don't mind,
But not eternally entwined!
That kiss! The costly price we paid
Resulted in the fire brigade:
Gnashing like a pair of nutters,
Freed at last by wire cutters.

What next?

My boyfriend's had his tongue stud done.
Magnetic tongues. That will be fun!

I'M NOT (A)CROS(TIC) WITH YOU AT ALL

Dear Richard, don't worry about the mess,
It was only my most expensive dress.
Can I meanwhile compliment you on your
Khaki pants and combat vest?
Phwooooar!
However, I have to say that despite
Envying your sense of style, I just might,
And I do hope this is OK,
Delay our next date for another day.

NO WAY

Can't stand him, I loathe him, detest and despise,
I hope he might meet an untimely demise.
Can't bear him, don't like him, I couldn't care less,
He's a nothing, a no one who doesn't impress.
Yet though he's as sexy as deep-frozen cod
He seems to believe he's a gift-packaged god.
I'm impervious now, he's a bucket of slime,
He can stick all his chat-ups where the sun doesn't shine.
A creep and a dull, insignificant bore,
A delusional git, self-obsessed to the core.
I'm a fool who just fell for his jet-propelled gob,
But this prince is a frog-featured, pond-dwelling slob.
He's a liar and scum-bag who said he would ring
But I bet he'll just boast of a one-night-stand fling.
He's a pus-bucket, a greaseball, a fatherless son (get it?),
Forget it, he's history, it's over and done.
I'd far rather spend lots more time on my own
Than waste any more thought . . . Oh, my God! It's the phone!
'Er . . . really . . . the party . . . enjoyed it . . . you what?
Tomorrow . . .? Well, maybe . . . Er, sure, yeah! Why not.'

DUMPED

My heart is playing truant since you dumped me.
Lessons yawn and hours drag their feet
Until I see you in the corridor
And I am a ghost, see-through.
Look! Put your hand in my chest and it's empty.

My tears got in trouble again,
Excluded from my eyes
At just the moment when everyone saw
And the class exploded in a laughing bomb.

Now,
My smiles skive off my face
And ugliness follows me like a shadow.
Falling in love!
Hah!
That's for swots of softness,
Teacher's pathetic pettings.
And love is a swear word,
Dug into toilet doors
And hope is in detention
Writing over and over:
    I won't do it again
    I won't do it again
    I won't do it again

FRENCH VERBS

Tomorrow, I will see him.
Erique. He will smile and
We shall sit together on the coach
To some historic castle.
We will be paired,
Like swans on a moat.

Today, we hold hands at the back,
Snatch moments in the shadows of stairs.
I bury my face against his scarf,
He whispers in French and I breathe him –
The smell of cigarettes, incense, vanilla,
Like autumn smoke.

Yesterday, he left.
Our breath froze as we said goodbye.
He gave me his scarf and half a pack of Gauloise
And we each kept a picture of us two
In the Boots photo booth.
As the coach pulled away,
The windows steamed up.
I could hardly see him wave
And the day was grey
As sackcloth.

UP FRONT

SCRITCH

This adjusting, done by boys
Is gross exhibitionism
It really annoys!

Now Bertie Horrocks liked a fiddle,
Gave his trousered bits a twiddle.
Cricketers rub and rap stars scratch
Their pocket billiards – game, sweat and match!
Justified young Bertie Horrocks,
As he played with Betty Swollocks.
He scraped by night and itchy day
Until he scritched himself away.
Next day he took a little peek
'Oh, woe!' He gave a high-pitched squeak,
He searched, but there was nothing there,
'Twas vanished into thinnest air . . .

The moral of this tale of Bert
Is that he got his just dessert:
Now he is worried, somewhat sick,
Has anyone out there Spotted Dick?

UNDER MY SKIN – SELF HARM

You laugh at me when I am quiet
Until I snap and round with spite on you;
Inside my veins, these feelings riot,
Course my blood and colour me blue.

Roll up my sleeve, see your name
Scribbled on skin with a pen
That uses blood. This is no game
Of words that cut again and again.

I score myself and plough my arm
For the bitter harvest. In this way
I garner glances of alarm-
Better than being ignored each day.

Some call this gouged graffiti cruel,
But I have learned these words at school.

BETRAYAL

Like rollerblades, we make a pair
Watch us practice; with such flair

Pavements fly beneath our feet
In this kingdom of concrete
The original polyurethane pals
Surfing down suburban hills
Gossip, giggle, God, it's great
To hang around with my best mate.

But my best mate's become a spy,
Sold my secrets. I blink my eye
And he has gone to the other side.
The gang ride by; I try to hide,
Cover my feelings with concrete.
As pavements fly beneath my feet

I climb the hills of hurt and hate
To get away from my best mate.

CRACKING NUTS

They call me **ill**,

The breakdown boy, you know, **one of them**

As they put their finger to their head

Twirl it like a gun,

To indicate I'm wrong.

And I am,

For in the morning when I wake,

There is no reassuring **this is day, get up, get on**

But just a heavy fear,

An out-of-focus, lack of grasp

And I am gasping for meaning.

Death, to this sixteen year old

Is round the corner, over the road. I take pills to hide

  His face,

But medication only slows . . .

I slur and stumble like a fool,

The jester who doesn't get the joke.

GOOD TO BE A LAD

Give us a bench on the pavement
That is home for the evening,
Where hours dawdle like shuffling shoppers
And we dine out on meaningless banter
Served with crappy lavatorial puns.
Let us hold serious debates
On midfield tactics, trainers to go into debt for,
Gadgets with overwhelming numbers of
    strange knobs,
Cars whose turbo thrusts punch holes in the ozone,
And top-ten lists of girls in Year 10.
Give us action movies where bad guys get it bad
And die in multiples of ten
And good guys kick huge arse, then get the girl.
And at last,
Give us late-night take-aways in a freezing square,
Each chip an instant hot-water bottle,
Savouring the good life, the smooth time,
The sweet hours
Of being a lad.

DISTANT SHORES

Don't pretend you understand,
Nod, or try to take my hand.
Don't patronise me with that look,
Say, 'I can read you like a book!'
You can't, not now, not then, not ever,
Believe me, you are not that clever.
'Teenage angst' is not my label,
I won't fit that tidy fable.
I'm in here and you're outside.
You're the cliffs and I'm the tide.
You don't know me any more,
To you I'm now a distant shore.
I stand alone on shifting sand
And you will NEVER understand.

ALL THE FUN
OF THE **FESTER**VAL

I live in the borough of **Acne**, Norf London

Wiv my **splatt**-mate

Who says every morning,

'Where'**zit** at?'

Yesterday,

When my **carbuncle** broke down,

I had to **pores** and think what to do.

Six **scabs** went by, but none stopped.

I was in a tight **spot,**

Bit of a **squeeze**

But finally caught the **pus** into town,

And went out for a lovely **pizza-face.**

SIZE MATTERS

I am treading water, just thirteen,
Drowning in a distinct lack of puberty,
Dreaming of armpit hair.
On this Californian beach
I am a swaying, skinny poplar
Surrounded by bronzed, bicep-bound oaks.
And every movie, magazine and myth I've seen
And read says
Boys like me don't get the girl,
But flounder about on the edge of the action.
And every movie, magazine and myth and
  boys' banter
In the shower room, behind the sheds, scribbled in
  stinking toilets
Says:
Size Matters.
And what they don't tell you in biology
Is that cold sea water
Shrinks even king-sized prawns to little shrimps.
But all these guys bouncing up and down this beach
Seem to have whole sperm whales packed away in
  their trunks.

And every crappy movie, dirty mag and lonely myth
Says:
I'm just small fry. And I believe the lie.
So today, instead of a gun,
I am packing a pair of socks.
As the waves crash,
I tumble and turn in this huge washing machine,
Hoping for no lost sock.

And for once,
When I stride from the surf
I'll sock it to 'em,
Win the battle of the bulge
And dream, dream, dream of growing up
To be like the movies and magazines and myths
  and men who say:
Size Matters.

SIZE MATTERS 2

I am a jellyfish stranded in the changing room,
Buffeted by the bustle of bristling bodies.
I shrink inside my faded orange bath towel
And hover in the slipstream of the shower queue.
Perhaps I won't be noticed
And the teacher will absent-mindedly assume I've
    just passed through.
But no, she's there, with register and pen,
Ticking one by one:
'Hang your towels on the hooks. Take your time.
The idea is to get clean,
Not see you if can dodge through without
    getting wet!'
She even keeps a list of 'dates'
To counter all the 'can't shower today, miss!'
    claims.
So, like sheep at the abattoir gate, each drops
    their towel and disappears,
Some blushing, some brazen.
My downcast eyes creep sideways:
'Oi! What you lookin' at? You a lezzie then?'
But every glance has only told me:
Size matters.

Shapes and curves easily defined as
'A cup', 'B cup' swell to
Defeat and deflate my double AAs.
'Fried Eggs!' laugh the boys in school,
'If you had no feet, you wouldn't wear shoes,'
They say, pinging the straps of my tiny bra.
And every joke, every up-and-down look repeats:
Size matters.

A few more shuffling steps.
My turn. Deep breath. Head down.
I close my ears to any shoals of giggles.
At least the fog of steam is welcoming.
I wrap myself in it
And dream that someone, someday shatters
The myth that:
Size matters.

SEX

ONAN THE BARBARIAN?

This isn't a sin,
And I find,
Such pleasure doesn't
Make me blind.

Wish I could
Believe the fact,
There's nothing sad
About this act.

Dress rehearsal
For someday,
By myself,
But that's OK.

PERFORMANCE PRESSURE

Raise a toast to the boast
You really should have done it
30 times down an alley
In the dirt lift the skirt
Against the wall, 30 seconds
That's all.
He lives for the boast in the boy's loo
Tell a tattle tale, is it true?
Do we care? Bin there,
And if you ain't, how very quaint and sad,
You'll never be a lad.
This is the pressure
Of the chat-up and the booze, cruise,
Dance-mix tricks,
The shout above the din,
Where you bin all my life?
Now you get it down yer neck
Til yer brain's a total wreck
It's a one-night fling –
Did he use anything?
Safe sex, what a joke,
He's the wham-bam bloke.

Be me, ah me, I ain't a he-man, man
Wanna wait for the date,
Listen to the word to get heard
In my heart make a start
With a flashing of the eye
In the night walk-talk.
Get to know each other in the flow
And there's plenty to do
Before we go all the way, no way,
Exploring with our hands
In different distant lands,
Betting on the petting
It's pleasure not pressure.
Raise a toast to the trust
That you don't need to do it 'til you're ready,
Take it steady
In the rhythm of love.

QUIZ YOURSELF

Considering the final move to prove your heart is his?
Grab a moment, have a break, take time to do a quiz.

YES NO
☐ ☐ Do you think you'll be more popular if
you go ahead?

YES NO
☐ ☐ Do you fear that you'll be left out,
if you don't leap into bed?

YES NO
☐ ☐ Do you want to seem more grown-up
and think he'll love you more?

YES NO
☐ ☐ Are you set on breaking age-rules
relating to the law?

Think you're ready? Really ready? Are you ready yet?
Feeling heady, going steady? On your marks, get set.

YES NO
☐ ☐ Has he said that if you loved him,
you would prove it, no delay?

YES NO
☐ ☐ Do you think he'll never leave you
if you answer right away?

YES NO

☐ ☐ Do you feel the label 'virgin' is uncool
and one to ditch,

YES NO

☐ ☐ In case you're labelled frigid, icy
maiden or tight bitch?

Think you're ready? Really ready? Are you ready yet?
Feeling heady, going steady? On your marks, get set.

YES NO

☐ ☐ Do your friends all boast about it,
keeping scores on endless dates?

YES NO

☐ ☐ Is it likely that your boyfriend wants
to brag to all his mates?

YES NO

☐ ☐ Does the thought of talking condoms
cause a blushing, cringe-reaction?

YES NO

☐ ☐ Does the issue of respect concern you
even just a fraction?

Time to count the scores now. Ready, steady, go?
If you've answered mainly YES, then consider saying NO!

THE NAMING GAME

Dick, tool, John Thomas, willy –
Inoffensive, even silly.
Nob, winkle, trouser snake –
Such names are not so hard to take.
Todger, wanger, words that lend
Humour to a man's best friend.
Vile expletives? Terribly lewd?
More of a giggle, not overly rude.

Now switch the gender, try to find
Which euphemisms spring to mind.
A dictionary won't help the hunt
For 'lady's bottom (at the front)'.

THE FARAWAY TREE

Back of car. Too far. Says who?
The mother whose car he's borrowed?
The father who told her to not be late?
But they love each other. Don't they?
And anyway it was really nice, sort of.
And it's not as though they hadn't talked
Or planned.
So why the breath of distance?
What they have done
Now hangs between them like laden branches.
Her grandad used to bring her walking here
And tell her of the Faraway Tree.

She traces a heart in condensation.
He stares at the steering column.
'So, you're OK? Did you . . .? Do you . . .?'
'Yeah, sure.' She turns and smiles,
Sees his jaw and hands unclench.
One arm closes round her while the other,
Clumsily in capitals, draws across the window:

I L♥VE YOU

'There,' he sighs. 'I mean it.'
And he does.

CONDOM

1.

That nervous night with you,
Unwrapped and willing to be worn;
Limp fears thrown aside
Clothing passion
With a glow.

2.

My brother scorns the rain,
Willing to bear the storm;
Consequence is hail
The size of sorrow,
And the scythe of the rainbow
Shall hunt him.

3.

There were nights
I threw the mad dice,
Risking all.
My luck held good,
But my brother, the gambler,
Has scattered his debt
In ashes.

THE RIVER

Takes him by the hand,
Upstairs to where she has hidden a river.
He almost stutters in her room, but she is gentle,
Helps him wade into the water. Hot.
She strips, dives under the duvet of dark.
And quickly, turning away,
Hiding his shame, he follows.
They kiss,
Her lips are waves running to the shore,
Their bodies are unsure,
Then touch with a ripple,
O the Oars stroking deep water now,
Where is the harbour?
Why doubt and fear this place?
As strong currents pull them
Down where feeling is all,
Rock the boat with smile and sigh
As he holds her and she holds him,
They are turning, tipping, river rushing in,
Over, yes overboard they sink but breathe underwater
And dying and living not drowning
No, no, this is air and another world

And perfect silence.

DRINK
and
DRUGS

OUT OF PUFF

When my lungs went on a protest march
To stop the torture;
When the fur coat on my tongue
Was sold at Sotheby's for ten grand;
When Laurence Llewellyn-Bowen
Tried to copyright the colour of my teeth;
When my breath got so bad
It was done for disturbing the peace;
When it took
One tent, two years' supply of Mars Bars
  and three teams of Sherpas . . .
To climb the stairs;
When I fell for cancer's crap chat-up line
and next thing I knew, he was all over me . . .
Then I finally sussed
I was a few fags short of a packet
And smoking (I'm not joking)

Was the habit to die for.

FIRST DRINK

There was a boy who was a boy
In the dark Slovakian night
Rasping on a rough tobacco
Dragging crows into his lungs
Coughing halos, burning now
For a drink to kill his thirst
It's his first, this two-pint glass
Filled with froth and foaming waves
He's a tide, he'll come on strong
Swallow down the spirit song
In a pub upon a hill
Wooden benches, starry roof,
Now he has his swaying proof
He tries to stand with all his will

But all of time is standing still, still
And he collapses, house of cards
As from his lips shoot shooting stars
Constellation of a spew
Blacking out, how he will rue
The day, oh rue the day
He drank his first drink, thirsty,
Cursing as he's carried home
To a cabin in the wood
Lay him softly on the bed
There was a boy, an English boy
Eleven years old with a mouth of gold
Tasting all his future fate
In the dark Slovakian night

IT'S LEGAL, SO THAT'S ALL RIGHT THEN

In the year 1990, in civilized UK,
Let simple death statistics have their say:
Cannabis – zero, ecstasy – three,
But thirty-thousand boozers in eternity.

Who comes top with the highest score?
Not smack at sixty-two or Methadone,
  eighty-four.
Guess who wins the kick-the-bucket bet?
At one hundred and ten thousand, it's . . .
  Mr Cigarette!

The politician says he understands,
But industry has tied his hands,
'Let's demonize drugs! But drink?
  Come off it!
Forget the principle, look at the profit!

'We need this tax, such welcome wealth
Covers the costs of our poor health
And being British, we'd surely miss
The blackouts, fights, the vomit and piss.'

GLUE

I have bought glue to stick together
What has fallen apart. Foul weather
Lends this concrete car park
A backdrop of dripping dumb down dark.
Time dawdles its frantic feet, drags
As we suck on plastic shopping bags
Breathe the fume that burns the brain.
Oblivious now to the singing rain,
We stagger down the echoing well
Under the weight of the sickening spell
Where clouds have stuck the sky together,
And broke our hearts in this foul weather.

VOMIT BLUES

Don't know about you
But when I've had a few
Have to head for the loo

With my palette of puke
It's a rainbow rebuke
From the diced-carrot duke

And no, I'm not thick
I'm the sultan of sick
And trickling's my trick

You think I'm a fool
Don't you know that it's cool
To dribble and drool?

So what If I sway?
It's so sexy to spray
And my mates go Wahay!

I'm the chairman of chuck
Yes, you'd better duck
From my fountain of muck

Now don't be a bore
As I fall through the door
Let's have just one more

I'm the alcopop king,
I slur as I sing
And athletically sling
With a:

Bleeeeeeeurrrrgh!

RECIPE for DISASTER

A pinch of fag smoke,
In fact, forget a pinch,
Think: empty the entire packet and slowly ferment
Whack in lashings of loud music
'til everybody's shaken and neighbours are stirred.
(Carefully remove parents beforehand)
In the meantime, you will need dough and a willing
  older sibling.
Mix in a dash of drinks that don't mix on empty stomachs
 (Especially the sweet strong stuff that makes insist
   isn't aimed at teens. My arse.)
  Add over-ripe cheesy chat-ups
    To spice up the proceedings
     Wait until the mix is slurry and blurry,
       Then stir your partner's mouth with your tongue
         (This is best done with a slow whisking motion
             With regular opportunities to come up for air.

However, boys should exercise caution
In case their mixture goes stiff.
This is a much later stage – see under PSHE).
Pour in a fumble of fairly innocent hands
(Again, below the waist is not a recommended recipe
As it will lead to a serving of 'Serves-You-Right-Slap-
   In-The-Face'),
Close windows and bake until one.
It is quite normal that the mixture now collapses,
Leaving a somewhat messy sleepover snog pudding
With snorers laid out like sponge fingers
Breath rising like yeast in the night.
The following morning expect headaches.
Add a soupçon of unexpectedly early-returning parents
To finish you off
When they go totally after dinner **mintal**.

This is **Cookery with Attitude**.

s
p
r
i
B
B
Like
Fly
Words
My
All
High
Now
Shy
Once
Shut
Science
Con-
Cut
Or
Mirr-
Need
My
Fill
Will
Speed
Of
Line
This

UP TO SPEED

THAT'S THE SPIRIT

This is:
Hand's best mate
Lip's kisser
Stomach's heater
This is:
Bottle's bottle
Nerve's distiller
Word's puller
This is:
Confidence kick-start
Tongue's turbo-charger
Flirt's fast car
This is:
Laughter's migration,
Chance's best chance
Late night's dreaming
This is:
Bladder's terrorist
Regret's lover
Head's Hammerer
This is
This is
This is

SORRY, AM I REPEATING MYSELF?

(A PANTOUM)

This dope is doing me in,
A somewhat squidgy black,
The jokes are a little bit thin
But we're having a giggle attack.

A somewhat squidgy black
It's going down a treat
We're having a giggle attack,
Now we need something to eat!

It's going down a treat
As we burgle the fridge for more
I still need something to eat,
Let us nip out to the store.

We burgle the fridge, what's more
The munchies have got us bad,
So let us nip to the store,
And see what fun's to be had.

The munchies have got us bad
And we stagger and sway in the street
Let's see what fun's to be had –
Oh, no, there's the Bill on the beat!

We try not to sway in the street,
But our paranoia's intense,
When stopped by the Bill on the beat,
Whatever we say must make sense!

Though our paranoia's intense,
He hasn't noticed, thank God
Whatever we said made sense!
And off he goes on the plod.

He hadn't noticed, thank God
The joke is now wearing thin
My brain is beginning to plod.
This dope is doing me in!

MAD FOR IT

I have gone mad, but we must stash this word,
The warmth of skunk, amphetamine thrill
And acid blur no longer work.
I have gone mad,
My mother leads me by the hand,
Prescribing doctors understand,
I swallow pills to numb what is already numb.
I have gone mad,
Such horrors flower in my head,
I must be confined to bed,
And on the ward,
I hear the schizophrenic screams.
My girlfriend comes, but as I shake,
She can no longer take
Such change in the laughing boy she knew.

Like shock, she pulls away,
And I am left with the long ache of day.
I have gone mad,
At school, the loony whispers grow,
Though some bring grapes,
Small bunches of love in their hearts.
Perhaps I shall grow well,
Today, I'm mad with me,
Believing every uttered lie
In the shallow cools of getting high.
How I shall miss the dealing out of
Sofa-sinking slur and sway.
But this was mad and made me mad
And on this psyche ward,
The breakdown lost-it elemental boy
Wonders if he has made a hash,
And searches, searches for the spirit's stash.

IT'S A SMALL WORLD

THE EGG PICKER-UPPER

Which came first,
The egg or the chicken?
Listen to this tale,
And let the plot thicken . . .

Once on the farm
The chicken scratched,
Found a barn
For eggs to hatch.

Eggs for chicks
And eggs on toast,
Chicken lived well,
A tasty roast.

The farmer smiled,
Though times were hard,
As bird ran free
Throughout the yard.

Times changed:

There was a man,
An egg-picker-upper,
He'd never again
Eat eggs for his supper.

Four thousand chickens,
All in one shed,
Some of them squawking,
Some of them dead.

Day was outlawed,
Lightbulb reigned,
Farmer vanished,
Birds well-trained.

Backs scratched raw,
Bleeding and sad,
This egg machine
Has gone quite mad.

And when their
Laying days have flown,
A pet-food tin
Is their final home.

The chicken, or the egg,
Which came first?
Who really cares,
For the bird that's cursed?

MINIMUM WAGE

Stood up
All day,
I earn the ache in my feet
And the cheap smile, stapled to my lips.
Today, some luck – a leftover lunch.
I sit outside the back door.
Four hours more,
Then bus to my bedsit
For food and sleep.
The boss drums on about teamwork –
I look at his suit and wonder.
We squabble over tip-division,
But a bit of a quid is sod-all.
The height of our shift
Is a stolen dessert.

When custom is quiet,
For a second, we breathe,
And I dream
Of more
Than the
Minimum.

1948 – OR ANY DATE IN THIS ISLAND'S HISTORY

I am not welcome,
That much is plain.
'No passport, no permit.'
I try to explain:

'My family's in danger,
My country's gone wrong,
My father's best friend
Was publicly hung!

'With his daughter
We were made
To dig the grave
In which he laid.'

The man's reply is:
'Are you a spy?'
His soul is suspicious,
His thin lips are dry.

All of us squeezed
Into one single room,
Layered like strudel
In the paraffin gloom.

I walk down the street.
A woman mutters:
'Do we need these
Foreign nutters?'

Romans, Vikings,
Celts and Jews,
All have sung these
Country blues.

Washed up on this
Island shipwreck
Register me as
Vera Fusek.

THE PROFESSOR OF PHILOSOPHY

We must stay! said the student,
And more was learned in a day,
Than all his lean years.
Posters were printed for the people.
But soldiers were kingfishers,
Darting through dissent.
They were swift, and his friends not quick enough.
He had the luck of the minnow.

That night,
He smuggled himself back to his father's house,
And did not leave for five forgetful years.
His mother, the cookery tutor,
Was happy to store him in the larder.
The father fabricated false partitions,
And the hours were slowly consumed.

By day, his father scoured libraries
And stole his boy an education.

By night, he crept into the living room,
Stuffed blankets into the piano
And forged his silent sonatas.

The country stopped.
Eyes and lips were careful.
Neighbours could be more than instruments
  of gossip.
Borders grew tight as drums,
Beating out the rhythm of the east.

Five years fled, like refugees.
His teeth rotted for lack of pantry-visiting dentists.
The train-dispatcher father
Built a coffin out of card,
Laid it in a bed of coal
And soused it in vinegar to put dogs' noses
  out of joint.

His son folded himself into that dark envelope,
Without a kiss.
The lid was sealed,
And as the steam train shuffled slowly West,
He wondered if success would always smell so sour.

PAPERS

The soldiers are working the café crowd
With pistols in belts and starched peak caps
It's easy to see: they are not nice chaps.
This fear in my stomach must not be allowed
To grow: 'Why are you here? When did you arrive?'
Our papers demanded, flicked through, checked,
They saunter away, our day out is wrecked
In Prague in 1985.

'We must not let these terrorists win!
Identity cards are worth the cost
Though civil liberties are lost,'
Reply our leaders to the din.

Stopped in the street: 'So who are you?'
United Kingdom, 2002.

POWERLESS OVER POLLUTION?

It began with a sweet wrapper, sailing through the sky,
But when I saw the look of envy in my mates, why
I knew I was on to something.
Soon fag packets were taking flying lessons
To the sighs of impressed girlfriends
And lager cans explored the principle of airborne navigation.
Things got a bit out of control:
Dealing chip papers, on windy street corners,
Inhaling car bonfires with a bad crowd,
Snorting while TVs fell from tenth-floor windows.
Eventually, we graduated to the heavy stuff –
I mean, all those politicians were up for it . . .
Injecting rivers,
Mainlining whole cities,
Overdosing on ozone holes.
Side effects? Countryside, animals, trees,
And a bit of a problem with oily seas.
It was a (poison) gas, the works, a total trip,
But in the end, a really rubbish relationship.

RED RIBBON – WORLD AIDS DAY

My ribbon is a
Twisted thread,
Woven for
The many dead:
Brother, sister
Lover, child,
Lives by this
Disease defiled.
With this ribbon
How we grieve,
But let us show
That we believe
This vein of life
Now running red
Links us in
A common thread.

PHARMA-SUIT-ICAL

Retrovirals? Rest assured,
If you are rich, you might be cured.
Research? Well, now, it costs a bomb,
Can't help every Hari, Dipna and Tom.
You say that we are not so nice,
But the poor must pay the price.
Protecting patents, that's the law –
Can't help the death of a few million more,
It's just business, don't you see?
Our shareholders would kill us! Honestly,
Where would the world be if we gave it away?
Here's some aspirin. Have a nice day.

FAMILY

THE PERFECT PICTURE OF TACTFULNESS

My girlfriend came round for a cup of tea,
Little sis butted in annoyingly,
'I tell you, I tell you, I tell you it's true –
Peter's got pictures of ladies like you
With no clothes on! They're under his bed!'
Silence falls. I wish I was dead.

FOR GRANDMA

Death has taken you, soft in your sleep,
Out of your hurting body, that much is true.
We are now the ones in pain, wondering why, as we weep,
Death has taken you.

Death, the breathless suitor, whispering 'I do'.
Mother of my mother said yes, grandfather's grief ran deep,
Husband no more to a bed-ridden bird that flew,

Flew to the far land, one of the countless many who
Were: father, brother, son – the quiet company you keep
There, where the dead in such sad interest accrue,
Death has taken you.

PETAL

My step-dad, soft as marigold petals,
Called me **his little girl.**
He built me a crab-apple tree house.
I left notes for the fairies,
Tested my bravery by jumping down.
He grew marrows, tomatoes, sweetpeas;
All was well in the garden . . .

I am fifteen and blooming.
Night falls,
Dark as black tulips.
His goodnight kiss,
planted on my mouth,
Has deeper roots.
He turns away,
Blindly turned on,
And my shock is a red poppy
In a field of grain
And all my love is battered by rain.

Dark Side

My
sister
curled up in
bed, skinny as a
sliver of moon.
When we were kids,
I was Dad's sunshine,
you – moonbean. But
some weird tide has
changed that happyfat
baby and in your room,
you snip at that photo
with scissors. Food has too
much gravity for you now.
At five stones, you say
you're in control, but your
eyes orbit strangely and your
body almost clanks. All the
magazines with their silver-
boned models, say it's 'lack
of self-esteem'. But our
home has always been
stuffed with love. You are
waning, almost gone from
the sky. When we were
young, I thought the
moon was made of
cheese... Our family
rises and falls with
your thin breath,
Oh my sister, my
crescent moon,
will you ever
be full
again
?

OUR STEVE

This place I remember
Smells unlike anywhere I know.
My feet have shrunk inside these shoes.
My shirt flaps
And my hands are the size of pillows
Stuffed awkwardly into pockets.

I am not a man here.
Even the chair is instantly familiar.
As I take a seat
Resisting the urge to tip it backwards,
'Mr Richards?' I say,
Hearing my voice escape like the pop of bubblegum.
A small frown pinches between his eyes
As he glances down his list.
'Sorry, you are ... ?' he asks.
'Here to talk about our Steve, 7R.'
I can feel sweat in the hollows behind my knees
As this man I know draws breath,
Still narrowing his eyes to fit my face.
He hasn't remembered yet.
Then he's off, telling me about
'Steve's prowess on the field'
And how he'd like him to try for the team.
He mentions casually how he'll need new boots
And the price of the kit.
I tell him I'll sort it,
And wonder silently about overtime.

He stops talking and looks at his watch

'Well ... Mr ... ?'

'Just one more thing,' I jump in,

'As his form teacher, could you...

Can you tell me how much homework he should be doing?'

He answers absently, 'About an hour a night',

Looking past me to see who's next.

'OK.' I nod quickly. 'Thanks.' And scrape the chair legs back.

It must be the sound that does it.

His eyes swivel sharply from my face to his list and back.

'Dan Carter!' his voice accuses,

And his finger tears holes in the silence.

'You're Steve Carter's brother!'

Like a stunned rabbit, I twitch

And try to mumble through a mouthful of old marbles.

'Good God, lad! I ... you ...'

He leans forward, eyes like searchlight.

'You were an absolute pain in the arse!'

And he shakes his head and then, unbelievably, smiles.

'So, Steve's your brother ...

Let's hope he doesn't go the same way, eh?'

I'm standing now

Feeling my shoulders inflate beneath my shirt.

'He won't,' I say,

'I'm making sure of it. That's why I'm here.'

And I wipe my hand down jeans

And slowly hold it out.

KNIFE SONG

The way this ends is not with a song,
For I dream of bringing my children along
The father sang as he sat alone
Hidden in his head
In the land of the dead
And the blade of the knife lay cold as bone.

I am the feather that fell from the goose,
Down and down now I have no use
The father sighed as he sat by himself
Hidden in his head
Dreaming of the dead
And the silent knife on the kitchen shelf.

In my belly is the setting sun,
Down, down to the darkness run
The father sighed as he sat with his wife
And how she wept
As his conscience slept
And night was falling on family life.

Take the children, tucked in bed,
Father's coming to do what he said
Hidden in his heart
Is a rusty dart,
But the beds are filled with pillows instead.

Oh, the father prayed to take them all,
But the house was hollow when he came to call
They are far away,
Where it's safe to play
The feather is plucked and ready to fall.

> *Driven, driven to the glade,*
> *To keep the promise that he made*
> Hidden in his head,
> His soul now led
> Down to the grove where he shall be laid.

The father whispered to the sky,
Grow me wings and I shall die,
Gripped the cable
As he was able
And like lightning learnt to fly.

> *Father slumped on the forest floor,*
> *Leaf that's fallen, and what for?*
> Hidden in death
> His last breath
> Shut for ever the hoping door.

Children safe, the mother sighed,
Broken like a cup inside
Happiness cracked
And heart attacked
For daddy-o-daddy-o-daddy-o's died.

SCATTERING THE ASHES

You have gone and all that is left is words
That ring like dull bells on my tongue
And my mouth is dry
As the ashes of your body.
For one whole year
We held you in a plastic bag;
You sat, airtight, in the living room of our mother's house,
Monolithic in your black-cornered container.

Easy to say the spirit had gone,
Jumping out from your body as the last breath exhaled.
Yet in those clustered granules
Were hands I held,
Rough scraping chin,
Your gangly angularities,
The dark eyes I begin to forget.

And so we took you, my brother,
Up on to the hill,
With scissors and bags and hands,
Ready to dip into you –
The bitterest sherbert.

We found an avenue of trees,
A lane of childish days
Where women with dogs avoided us,

The weeping mother,
The cold-eyed son
Unable to comprehend the vastness of his grief.
We scooped you up
To place you at the beginning of each trunk,
An offering, a grey sacrifice,
And my mother, laden with the years,
The endless avenue of deaths,
Fell to the grass and cried out
At this ancient and Greek tragedy,

We stumbled home to finish the job
Of spreading my brother out
In the places we best remembered:
One for the wasp nest,
One for the pear tree,
One for the feast,
One for the fire,
One for the den,
One for the cut-down willow,
Where we played the perfect game of hide-and-seek.

You are hidden now,
Cut down in the maleness of your days.
My mother is made grey
By your ashes
And your terrible gift to me
Is an oldness in my youth
And the heaviness of these words
That ring like dull bells on my tongue.

A PERIOD COSTUME DRAMA

Boyfriend round for cup of tea,
Brother enters 'look at me!'
With bullet belt and cowboy hat –
But, oh my God, what the hell is *that?*
'I found these bullets by your bed,
But each one has a stringy thread . . .
Is that where the fuse is lit?'
Enquires the brainless little git.

Oh! This life is much too cruel,
As boyfriend falls right off his stool.
There must be ways I can get rid
Of Little Bruv, The Tampon Kid.

JUST

It was **just** a dare.

It was **just** wanting to be part of the gang.

It was **just** a packet of sweets.

It was **just** not quite quick enough.

It was '**Just** where d'you think you're going with
that?'

It was **just** a call to the police

It was **just** terrifying.

It was **just** after midnight when Mum and Dad
came

'**Just** a youngster!' they pleaded

It was **just** a caution, at last.

It was **just**ice, I guess.

It was ' **just** wait 'til you get home!'

It was going to be just like always – unfair, un **just.**
But

It was '**Just** come here, stupid!'

And after the shouting and tears, **just** a warm hug

'**Just** don't do it again, see?'

It was **just** family.

SCHOOL

DREAMING

I am a fat, curled-up comma,
Waiting in the library
And outside
The gang,
With fists full stopping at my face.
But here, I am the page
In a kingdom of words.
I catalogue the flutter of leaves
In this thought-forest.

In my head is an unwritten romance
Where ample girls are adored by men with huge
Intellects.

Now, I pause, for the singing of the bell
And the rush of gabble, gob and
gossip.
I swing into silence,
Through the long sentence of
streets
To curl up at last,
In the unhappy ending of
Home.

BALLAD OF MATT THE KNIFE

Why, oh, why did I carry a knife?
Because I was so scared for my life.
How I strutted the cruel school yard,
Bigger than the bully boys hard.

They beat me 'til I was blue and black,
My bloody nose and tooth for the crack.
But I'm a firework, watch me flare,
Now, I wonder, will they dare?

DID I-DID I-DIDDLE-I-DIE,
SHARP AS HATE AND CLEVER AS A LIE.

Then there came, there came a day,
When we put childhood away,
Tattle taunts and treasure toys,
This is the moment, come on boys!

Light the match, and stand well back,
I'm fizzing, ready to attack.
Incandescent Roman candle,
My revenge too hot to handle.

DID I-DID I-DIDDLE-I-DIE,
SHARP AS HATE AND CLEVER AS A LIE.

The fuse is lit and from each pocket,
Flies a silver-bladed rocket,
Now you'll find out how I feel,
We circle like a Catherine wheel.

Bang like a banger! Dance, he's down,
I wear the victor's sparkling crown.
But, what's this? I stagger in pain,
As from my chest flows golden rain.

DID I-DID I-DIDDLE-I-DIE,
SHARP AS HATE AND CLEVER AS A LIE.

Nothing sorted, nothing solved,
The fun and fury has dissolved,
Watch me fall without a shout,
On the ground, I am burnt out.

This bloody ballad of the knife
That did not save but snatch my life,
See my mother, father cry,
For their son, the bonfire guy.

DID I-DID I-DIDDLE-I-DIE,
SHARP AS HATE AND CLEVER AS A LIE.

IT'S ALL IN A NAME

(True story from a teacher who thought she heard a rude word)

There once was a pupil called Kerr
To whose parents it did not occur,
That naming him Wayne
Was somewhat insane,
And his classmates concurred, with:
Wayne Kerr!

MOOS AT TEN

Listen lads and understand,
This lighting of farts is well out of hand.
A scientific experiment, Shane?
To prove that cows produce methane?
How now, the poor brown cow
Light the match and BIFF! BANG! POW!
It's enough to make you wince
The sight of instant frying mince,
In fact, miss, I must agree,
It was an *udder* tragedy.

CAT'S CRADLE

I hate you and you hate me,
And though you're prettier than I,
It's not so simple. Don't you see?

We were best friends in Primary
But when I ask the stupid question why
I now hate you and you hate me,

You reply: 'Silly cow! That's history!'
It makes me want to cry:
'It's not so simple'. But you don't see,

No, you'd rather snog the boy I fancy
And give me the finger. I could die.
I hate you and you hate me.

Our screaming fights, though quite fist-free,
Scrape nails down cheeks as insults fly:
'You simple bitch!' And we don't see

The sudden arrival of the deputy.
Detention is nothing. I'll get by.
I hate you and you hate me.
It's that simple. Don't you see?

MR ROGERS

Let's set the scene – it was Hallowe'en
Hanging out in the rec, feeling blue
And bored out of our skulls, nothing to do,
Remembered Mr Rogers, for a dare,
Egged each other on to give him a scare.
Bought a bunch of eggs from the corner store,
With Hallowe'en masks, we knocked on the door.
One of the gang screamed 'Trick or Treat!'
Then we scrambled down the street,
But not before we managed to get
A Mr Rogers Omelette!
He went ape, it was great for the crack,
The night we launched our egg attack.

It was just for fun, we're not that cruel,
But we haven't seen him since in school.
Just a tasteless little yolk,
Can't Mr Rogers take a joke?
Next time, no treat, we'll try the trick
Of smashing his windows with a brick.

MR ROGERS 2

Too busy marking, I hadn't seen,
That once again it was Hallowe'en.
Up all night, feeling blue,
Working in the living room, as you do.
You start to wonder, What's the point?
I had reached my boiling point,
Twenty years, I've given this school,
I care about my kids, I must be a fool,
That night, quite late, the buzzer went,
Opened the door to my lads hell-bent
On treating me to their idea of a joke.
'Let's get the fat bloke!'
They chanted as they chucked their eggs,
Then ran away as fast as their legs
Could carry them. Now, I'm a mess,
Suffering from stress-related illness.
I couldn't face my class next day.
I ask you, what would I say?
Thanks to a single violent spell,
I've learned to hide inside my shell.

THE NIGHTHAWKS (AFTER EDWARD HOPPER)

This little harbour
Where bored pupils moor their boots
In the faggy mist.
School is forgotten now,
Stubbed out
As we dawdle and drag.
Trawling for laughter,
Our words are puffed out
Or held in the heart
Expelled in perfect gossiping rings.

Through the window,
In the streets,
Afternoon spills into evening
A rush-hour tide of flowing feet and faces.
The moon is a silver spoon.
Lights come on in the café.

Every word has been said now.
The chink of cup and spoon is done
As we fumble for change
And disperse like sugar
Dissolving into the caffeine city
With peppermints handy for questioning parents;
But for the moment we are sails,
Filled up with ourselves
Heading homeward
Through the dregs
Of dusk.

NOTES
FOR THE
READER

Some of the poems in this collection are based on personal experience and others (including some of those written in the first person) were inspired by listening to young people tell their own stories.

FORMS

There are many different forms of poetry used. Some of the more complex forms are explained below. Others can be looked up in a dictionary.

- Free verse – *Skate Date* (page 108), *Size Matters* (page124), *Size Matters 2* (page 126).

- Couplets – *Within Spitting Distance* (page 103), *The Perfect Lad* (page 107), *No Way* (page 113).

- Puns – *All The Fun Of The Festerval* (page 123) is squeezed full of tabloid-style groanworthy wordplay.

- Acrostic – *I'm Not (A)cros(tic) With You At All* (page 112).

- Performance and rhythm – *Performance Pressure* (page 130).

- Ballad – *Matt the Knife* (page 180). This poem, like many ballads, has been set to music. It was inspired by tragic events in the news, and recollections of teenage fights.

- Villanelle – *Cat's cradle* (page 183). This form of repeated lines echoes the unending and bitter feuds that can destroy school years. Tercets with a quatrain (four-line stanza) finish. The rhyme scheme is ABA ABA ABA ABA ABAA. The first and third lines of the first stanza are repeated at the end of each stanza in different order until the last quatrain, where these two lines make up the final couplet.

- Shape poems – *Up To Speed* (page 148), *Dark Side* (page 168).

- Sonnet – *Under My Skin – Self Harm* (page 118). Andrew met this girl briefly while working in a school. Without thinking, she had rolled up her sleeve, revealing the dreadful gouges in her arm.

- Roundel – *For Grandma* (Andrew's grandmother) (page 166). Made up of three tercets on two rhymes with a repeated refrain, this form reflects the circularity of life and death.

- Extended metaphor – *Petal* (page 167) uses the imagery of flowers.

- Pantoum – *Sorry Am I Repeating Myself?* (page 150) This poem is made up of quatrains with lines two and four in stanza one repeated as lines one and three in stanza two and so on. The final stanza puts lines one and three of stanza one as lines two and four. The pattern of repeating lines mirrors the state of mind.

PERSONAL NOTES

French Verbs (page 115) is based on Polly's French exchange experience.

Quiz Yourself (page 132) is loosely based on an actual teen magazine quiz.

The Naming Game (page 134) – This poem is based on the sexism of expletives.

Many of the poems in the DRINK AND DRUGS section are based on Andrew's teenage years. *First Drink* (page 140),